Disrupt the Status Quo:

Living and Leading from Your Success Zone

By Aimée V. Sanchez, Ph.D.

DEDICATION

This book is dedicated to the most important people in my life that have been critical to my success. With great appreciation I dedicate this work to my husband and best friend, Pastor Louie Sanchez. Without your love and support this book would not have been possible. To my children Micah and Madison, you constantly remind me to laugh and enjoy life; you two remain my motivation to continue to pursue my best self. I also want to thank my sister Tiffany, you are such a huge support to me, and I thank you for being my confidant. To my Aunts

Betty and Bertha, and, my entire Vickers Family you all have encouraged and inspired me to lead, live, and love from the heart. To my parents the late Mr. & Mrs. Jimmie L. Vickers you raised me to stay hungry for the truth, to embody strength, and to acknowledge my power- you believed I was born to influence. To Linda Sanchez thank you for being my mother, and for loving me unconditionally. To my spiritual advisors and Pastors Johnny and Susie Mendez, thank you for your counsel, your love, and your trust. I thank you for allowing me to lead and serve alongside you at Crosspoint Church. I also thank all of the individuals who have prayed with me and supported me in pursuit of my goals. I remain grateful to God for allowing me to pursue my passion and vision for my life. I am humbled by my calling to serve and lead others, and am committed to the great commission (Matthew 28:19-20).

CONTENTS

"The function of leadership is to produce more leaders, not more followers"

- RALPH NADER

As a child I was raised to be independent, strong minded and forward thinking.

Sometimes it meant that I embarked on endeavors alone because my counterparts found the venture too risky.

I believe I possess many of those same traits as a leader today in that I am always striving to improve and am willing to take the risk of investing in growth for the cause of the greater good.

As a leader we are called to a higher sense of responsibility.

What type of legacy has your leadership birthed?

INTRODUCTION

I decided to write this book as a personal testimony and challenge to you, the aspiring leader or high performance professional that is currently on the rise, to find the courage to Live and Lead from your Success Zone. Part of being able to successfully shift your mindset from that of 'goal focused' to 'success oriented' is being able to first acknowledge that something needs to change.

In my over 20 years of experience working with individuals and within organizations building and strengthening teams, I have found that people often ask me; "how do you do it?" which means: "how do you remain laser focused on meeting organizational goals and still remain true and authentic to who you are?"

This answer is complex and comes from many years of trying to do it in ways that ultimately didn't work for me. Overall, the approach required is a holistic one that takes into account how you function as an individual in every aspect of your life, and it requires that you remain attentive to your individual needs for happiness and success in all areas of life, including personal, professional, spiritual and physical. The balance comes from a primary focus on managing your individual energy and not the environment that you are a part of.

What my experience has taught me is that there are a set of critical characteristics, traits, habits, and performance standards that high performing top producing professionals must adhere to in order to excel, to be *great*, and to truly stand out in the professional world. Observing the performance standards of other successful individuals is an excellent way to achieve the lifestyle of a high performing professional, because yes, there is a *lifestyle* that you must adopt in order to reach greater success.

I've written this book to help guide you on your journey towards acquiring the characteristics and behaviors necessary to achieve your vision for success. These strategies require practice, patience, and commitment to your final goal. There is nothing new or innovative described here. These strategies have been discussed and utilized by many successful people before you. The challenge comes in successfully applying the right strategies in order to achieve success.

Think of this process as a continued investment in your *journey of development.* And, consider this *your training*; a training that will help in a number of ways such as: helping you grow as a leader, helping you to take a closer look at the way you do things, helping you become increasingly efficient, and helping you question what you know.

So, right from the start, I'm going to ask some questions to stimulate your thought process. Continue to think about these questions as you advance through this book.

How much do you love your job?

Do you end each workday feeling fulfilled?

Are you confident that you are in the right position with the   right company?

Are you focused on activities that matter to you?

Are you capitalizing on your strengths?

Are you effective and realizing your full potential?

Are you having any fun?

Do you know that for a majority of individuals, the answer to these questions is an absolute "No!" I remember seeing an episode of Oprah maybe about 20 years ago and she was talking about the importance of finding your passion in what you do. I used to think that was such a ridiculous concept, but maybe that was because of my maturity level at the time. As a young professional, I was more focused on the things that I thought would grant me the success and happiness that I wanted in my profession. Things like position, title, salary, material things, the type of home I owned, if I was married, and where my children went to school. I envisioned a job as a direct pathway to those things. I saw the job as an instrumental, or a tool to achieving my vision of success. I didn't make a connection necessarily between my core values and my ultimate goal. I remember that what really impressed me about that Oprah episode was that there was a man who said that he went to work every day and hated his job. I couldn't fathom how he could hate his job and still go to work everyday? I thought, "why torture yourself?" It seemed like the ultimate slow death to me.

But unfortunately, not everyone feels as

though they have the options or opportunities to come out of a job that they dislike in order to do something else. Some others enjoy the job, but dislike the burden that the organization imposes on them doing their job. A 2013 Gallup poll indicated that two thirds of employees are disengaged at work or worse. Other research conducted supports the notion that, of the country's approximately 100 million full-time employees; 51 percent aren't engaged at work -- meaning that they feel no real connection to their jobs, and thus they tend to do the bare minimum. Another 16 percent are 'actively disengaged' - they begrudge their jobs, tend to complain to co-workers and drag down office morale as a result. Other factors that might affect employee satisfaction and engagement might be: job enlargement (your job continues to expand because you are getting additional tasks, in addition to your job - it just keeps increasing), having a negative or unsatisfactory relationship with your superiors or management, information overload, the pace of change, constant demands for instant service, downsizing, rightsizing, globalization and advances in our new knowledge-based economy. Whatever the reason might be, far too many of us are feeling burned out, stressed out, and maybe even disengaged by the daily grind. Therefore, many people are living their lives in tormented mediocrity, desperately trying to escape failure.

You might be asking, how do you effect positive and sustainable change in a climate of this kind? I think the answer could be that organizations, leaders, and those that have influence need to determine that strengths are important, and that playing to the strengths of each individual maximizes overall effectiveness. Working from a strengths-based model of leadership, one can also meaningfully identify their own areas of weakness and discover how to multiply their effectiveness.

Overall, the idea is for transformational leadership to replicate leaders, and to expand their sphere of influence. This is best done by coordinating teams of individuals that are clustered around their own individual strengths, thereby, being able to as a team effectively leverage other's challenges or weaknesses. Additionally, one of the operating expectations within a group of this type is to catapult growth for both the individual and the organization. Many people get frustrated because they feel unable to discern and optimize their individual strengths. These people eventually burn out as they become exhausted with pushing back against environmental demands, added expectations, and ultimately become overwhelmed with the search for meaning and relevance. These might appear to be people who seem ill- suited to their jobs in one way or another. They may be present every day, but they are absent in mind. Ultimately, this mindset results in them not being engaged, invested, or committed.

"If your actions inspire others to dream more, learn more, do more and become more you are a leader."

- JOHN QUINCY ADAMS

When I look back over my life I feel so blessed to have been influenced by leaders who were willing to take the time to invest in me. They each had my admiration not just because they took the time to add value to my journey, but also because they each spoke the truth into me about who I was going to be. They could see things about me that I couldn't see in myself. They put words to my potential and told me that it was infinite.

I believed them however, because I was so inspired by how they lived their own passions. Their models of Leadership were bold and rich with purpose. For me, it was easy to envision living a life of purpose when I could see others whom I admired doing it every day.

What do your actions as a leader say to others?

My story...

I have spent a substantial part of my career working in the Corporate arena, in addition to maintaining a separate and successful Psychology Practice devoted to assessment. Although I believe that I entered many of these organizational settings with the mindset of an entrepreneur, I very much understood the Corporate organizational structure and the demands placed both upon management and employees. However, what I found was that try as I could, I too became engaged in the mission of the organization, and I too became frustrated by many of the systemic challenges that caused stagnation within the organization.

Many of the situations that both employees and management complained about often resonated with me. I witnessed first hand the dedication of the staff and the management to fulfilling the organizational mission. However, from my perspective there appeared to be a number of recurrent challenges, such as:

1. The system was highly complex, and processes for implementation were often disjointed.

2. The continuously high demand work environment resulted often in high burnout.

3. The organizational procedures were

overladen with urgent processes that were continually changing and were not always readily verifiable. Therefore, on a daily basis this meant that the productivity of the employees was often interrupted. Additionally, employees remarked that constant interruptions clouded their individual abilities to find meaning in their work.

4. Employees were intermittently engaged and often did not want to deal directly with management.

5. The organization had multiple missions that were being pursued on a frequent basis, and employees could not keep up with the changes or trainings to incorporate innovations or new

procedures.

6. The organization fostered a fear-based mindset.

7. The organization didn't focus on professional growth, but   instead focused on mandatory trainings.

8. At one point there was up to a 50% turnover rate, and a 40% functional vacancy rate. But no one asked why.

I would love to be able to say that despite all of these challenges, we experienced no failures. But that wouldn't necessarily be true. My role often was to help coordinate with individual teams and management to efficiently execute many of these missions. We always delivered. However, there were some losses along the way that added to the complexity of the situation. Many of these, were not always within our span of control due to the policies and procedures of the organization, such as:

1. People may have been brought onto a complex project (without consulting the specific management team) based solely on internal recommendations. In about 20% of the cases, the individual ultimately was determined not to have been a good fit for the position (i.e. quality and quantity of work was not what was expected, or the employee did not have the level of expertise needed to work independently in the position).

2. Too large a workload may have been compressed onto too few people due to their abilities to manage the job in comparison to underperforming peers.

3. Due to the disjointed management structure of the organization, some subcontractors were able to freewheel because proper controls were not put in place.

4. Employees were not always provided proper notice about trainings, changes in mission, or procedures to execute daily tasks. Therefore, employees were unsure about how to proceed.

After witnessing this for so long, it became uncomfortable to continue to watch the process be replicated over and over again. As a result, I became sometimes the only person that would challenge or ask the following questions every time there was a change in mission, such as:

Why are we doing this?

What needs to change?

What does it cost us not to change?

Who does this change impact and how?

What do we stand to profit or gain if we change?

Is this change in line with our core mission?

Sometimes I would receive a worthwhile response, but many times the overwhelming answer was, "this is our culture, this is how we do it" or "we have to do this because this is the direction we have been given". Overtime, continuing to focus upon asking management these questions and waiting for the answers helped to provide clarification regarding the urgent need for change. Additionally, this line of questioning began to prompt those in leadership to hold an intentional discussion that involved the impact of their decisions upon their employees.

Eventually, I was able to continue to work directly with senior management and those from headquarters to continue to dialogue directly regarding many of the decisions before they were executed. As a result, some unnecessary processes were halted. However, old habits are hard to change. Those same patterns continued to repeat themselves, and although my team and I were able to successfully execute each complex program mission change; it eventually took a toll on the employees and me as well, frankly.

One day, 'the work' just became 'that work', and it was no longer fun. I found that my commitment wavered when two critical things happened: (1) The meaningfulness of the work was no longer there, and (2) I felt as though I was no longer able to bring value to the organization or those over whom I had an influence.

This realization caused me to revisit my own path to personal development and fulfillment, which I started on 20 years before, and I began to read as much as I could on the topic. I found myself reading material from some of the most innovative thought leaders in the world, such as John Maxwell, Brian Tracy, Les Hewitt, Dr. Richard Barrett, and Jack Canfield to name a few.

In 'The Power of Focus' by Les Hewitt, a top business and personal development coach he talked about 3 critical factors to improving focus on your life goals such as:

Establishing clearly defined and measurable goals with a defined timeline.

Working toward the realization of these goals.

Ensuring a balance in all areas of your life.

What was critical for me at this time was that I felt as though the balance in my life was missing and that I had lost focus. Les Hewitt's book helped me to get a better sense of my personal and professional priorities. Another book that I read which was extremely valuable to me was John Maxwell's book, 'The 21 Irrefutable Laws of Leadership'. In it, he talked about 'the

Law of the Lid' and about leaders needing to raise their level of effectiveness by understanding their own strengths and weaknesses. Additionally, he challenged leaders to utilize this approach when leading others and encouraged them to take ownership of identifying and building the strengths and weaknesses of the members of their teams. I knew that going forward I would continue to challenge myself to grow, but also that my charge was to be available to help others grow as well.

However, to earn the credibility and permission to lead others to growth you must first have their trust. With trust lacking, there is resistance to creativity, freedom, and exploration. Much like the organization that I spoke about, a fear-based culture is the opposite of a creative, thriving and trusting environment. When a team is unable to achieve this level of internal cohesion within the work environment, it means that people are never really able to be at their best. They are often holding back and are not free to explore. The other critical factor to successfully building trust comes from focusing on the culture of the team or the organization. For example, if the culture is fear-based, the focus is fear. In a fear-based culture, you will not have a thriving or winning enterprise. The culture will ultimately define a leader's success.

As a transformational leader, being able to set the culture is pivotal to being able to maintain employee engagement. As a leader Living and Leading from Your Success Zone, you realize that organizational transformation first begins with the transformation of the leaders; because the culture of an organization is actually a reflection of the mindset of those in leadership. When a leader is willing to be aware and take ownership, they have decided to set the culture. So, in essence, if there is going to be transformational change for an organization, one of two things have to happen, either the culture changes or the team changes.

You might ask; "how do you ascertain that your interventions for change have been successful?"

Well, depending on what your focus is, you can measure so many different things. But realize that the culture sets the standard. If your standard becomes that of innovation, creativity, high performance, employee satisfaction, this will be reflected in your relevant performance markers. However, if the culture is that of fear, where the focus is primarily results-oriented; then, the data will support that as well. Primarily with regards to employee satisfaction, engagement, turnover, sick time usage, etc. Again, organizational transformation begins with the leadership. If the leaders don't change, then the culture remains stagnant and won't change. Therefore, organizations must be invested in growing and developing their leadership as well as their staff.

In the book, Corporate Culture and Performance, authors John P. Kotter and James L. Heskett indicate that companies with solid adaptive cultures based on common or shared values outperform other companies by a significant margin. Also, they found evidentiary proof over an eleven- year period that the companies grew four times faster than others when they demonstrated care for all stakeholders in comparison to companies that did not share these values. Other benefits included: job creation rates that were seven times higher, stock prices that matured twelve times faster, and a profit performance ratio that was 750 times higher than companies that did not have shared values and/or adaptive cultures.

Similar findings in other research supports the view that companies that consistently maintain a culture which is focused on building strong values and remain values driven outperform companies that do not maintain that position. Additionally, care for all stakeholders (i.e. leadership, employees, customers) also contributes positively to the overall bottom line (Jim Collins and

Jerry Porras, 1994; Rajendra S. Sisodia, David B. Wolfe, Jagdish N. Seth, 2007).

Dr. Richard Barrett founder of the Barrett Values Centre commented in a 2010 article titled, "The Importance in Building a High Performance Culture," that a paradigm shift with regards to the perception of values in the organizational and leadership arenas is urgently needed. He opines that full range awareness and values alignment are emerging as the most significant factors in predicting organizational success. As research has demonstrated, companies that emphasize shared focus on their values often outperform companies that do not. Additionally, these companies have been shown to exceed standard markers for resilience, sustainability, and success in comparison to other companies. However, this type of success becomes possible only when leaders acknowledge the importance of creating an organizational culture that continually advances and matures to serve the needs of all stakeholder groups.

The Barrett Values Centre is leading the industry with regards to values-based assessment of organizations and leaders. They utilize a constellation of assessment tools, called the Cultural Transformational Tools (CTT), which assess and map the underlying factors that promote or inhibit performance. The instrument's uniqueness lies in its focus on an individual or organization's motivating values that are a reflection of stated needs.

In my practice, I utilize a number of assessment procedures for evaluating individual and organizational change. Many of the assessment procedures include tools that address organizational culture, values identification, personality, and leadership characteristics. The results of these types of assessments are critical in being able to clarify areas where growth or improvement is needed. Additionally, when working with teams and organizations to explore culture transformation, I assess the importance of values and it's alignment with the core mission.

Often, I challenge leaders to come back to the questions that I outlined earlier, because they bear similarities with regards to those that concern culture transformation. I encourage leaders to ask themselves and their counterparts:

Why are we doing this (i.e. setting the culture)?

What needs to change about the culture?

What does it cost us not to change the culture?

Who does this culture change impact and how?

What do we stand to profit or gain if we change the culture?

Is this culture change in line with our core mission?

The title of this book came to be because I found myself being the person that was continuously showing up dissatisfied with the status quo. I realized that although the organization often had much to do with fostering an environment settled in routine, the most critical take away for me was that I realized that I could not feel fulfilled, or as though I was truly reaching my full potential in an environment in which I was comfortable with maintaining mediocrity.

When we talk about Living and Leading from Your Success Zone, this zone of success is ultimately a journey not just a destination. However, what I've discovered is that to embark on this journey fully, one typically must be willing to evaluate where they currently are with regards to three zones. Typically, individuals whom I coach will progress through these three phases in their own process of evolving towards achieving personal and professional success:

1) The Learning Zone: In this zone you are learning a thing for the first time, you have a task that you haven't performed before and therefore, you remain open to learning because everything is new. As a leader, learning to adapt in the learning zone yields the highest return, because you remain teachable in your mindset and are able to incorporate and integrate changes that will spur your learning process. In this stage you challenge yourself to grow.

2) The Comfort Zone: In this zone, it is just as it sounds, everything is comfortable, you've settled in. For the learner, you have now mastered learning, and have acquiesced to the status quo. In this zone, you don't seek out change, adaptation, or modification; you want to keep things on a routine schedule. In this zone as a leader, you are not challenged, you do not stretch; your growth has plateaued.

3) The Drifting Zone: In this zone, I think of the movie 'The Fast and The Furious." In that movie the drivers would utilize a driving technique called drifting. Drifting refers to a driving technique where the driver intentionally over-steers, causing loss of traction in the rear wheels, while maintaining vehicle control and a high exit speed. Just like a powered muscle car that has to be forced to induce a drift; the drifting zone describes an intentional effort to remain in the present state. The leader is coasting off the success of the previous zone. In this zone, the leader has 'mastered the drift.' Again, they aren't challenged, aren't stretched and can't see future success. The goal in this zone is to remain under the radar.

But there is one last stage, a fourth zone, which I like to call the zone of disruptive momentum (DM). In this zone, as a leader, you're dissatisfied with the status quo, and have made it your responsibility to challenge the paradox of mediocrity. In the zone of DM, you and I realize that we have a responsibility to lead and live from a state of disruptive momentum. Meaning, we believe that the decisions that we make, the questions that we ask, and the boundaries that we challenge will disrupt the momentum of routine life...it is a state that requires that we do more, not less. I hope that's you. I know that's me.

Francisco de Souza, the CEO of Cognizant Technology Solutions, says; "In today's era of volatility, there is no other way but to re-invent. The only sustainable advantage you can have over others is agility, that's it. Because nothing else is sustainable, everything else you create, somebody else will 'replicate." I love this quote, because it in essence describes shattering the comfort zone and requires that one becomes an active participant. To be a game changer, you realize that remaining in limbo and in a state of inactivity is not a good place to be. Companies that become resigned to the status quo risk becoming irrelevant, obsolete and extinct. Winning enterprises must seek to continually live in their zone of disruptive momentum (DM) by frequently questioning the predictable, reinventing work, and welcoming disruptive advances. In essence, if you're going to be an enterprise that wins, thrives, survives, and stays alive you've got to get uncomfortable!

As leaders with influence, we need to realize that in order to be successful at leading others, and maintaining our own credibility as leaders, we need to ask ourselves difficult questions and be ready to accept and hear the answers. So, what zone best describes what stage you're living out of ? Are you in the learning zone? Are you living out the comfort zone? Or, have you mastered the drift and you are living out of the drifting zone?

As a leader, your biggest impact is with those whom you lead. If you are a leader and you aren't able to provide an answer to these questions, then ask yourself why? The reason I say this is because if you have not identified what zone you're living in, then your growth becomes limited by this blind spot. Essentially, you limit your ability to see a way forward with regards to your own growth which results in an inability to sustain change in behaviors that could be holding you back from advancing to the next level in your performance. Additionally, for those whom you influence, your contributions to their growth are limited and less meaningful because you have a skewed perspective.

No matter where you are, what team you're on, or what client you're working with, you need to lead others to help them understand where they are living, and which zone they are living in. We can't get to the zone of DM until we understand fully, the challenges of the learning zone, the comfort zone, and the drifting zone. I'll say it plainly here, you can't lead what you haven't lived!

For example, in the learning zone, your team or your client will continue to try new things. They will explore and sometimes they will fail, but, the beauty of this stage is that failure is a viable option.

In this zone, failure is not final, and is instead considered to be critical to cementing the learning process. Failure is actually considered a catalyst to growth. In this zone, one is inspired to grow by embracing the concept that 'to achieve something of an exceptional nature, it is inevitable that you will try something new'. In this zone, there is an inherent acceptance of risk, and one has to be willing to go out on a limb even if it means that you have to start over again.

While, in contrast to the comfort zone; the challenge becomes being too comfortable. As a leader, some of the individuals you lead may make an intentional effort to remain nested in the comfort zone because they are fine with the no risk factor. What I mean by no risk is that the results are reproducible, predictable, and the individual knows that what they have is a no-harm-guaranteed-plan for producing average and routine. This can show up in our work environments or in how we lead. This might be observed in an organizational sense with individuals who hold the perspective that organizational culture and norms can't be changed and aren't worth shaping or modifying. Therefore, the individual possesses no desire to challenge the status quo, which can have deleterious effects on the creative atmosphere of the organization.

Organizational culture in and of itself is not wrong or even problematic until it begins to stall creativity and create a burgeoning downward spiral towards mediocrity and irrelevance. Elon Musk the PayPal and Tesla founder was quoted as saying; "the problem is that at a lot of big companies, process becomes a substitute for thinking. You're encouraged to behave like a little gear in a complex machine". When the rigidity of culture is so restrictive that it negatively impacts the bottom line, it becomes something that is worth taking a closer look at. In an effort to maintain culture, many people may minimize the need to create challenges, or to take risks because it goes against the culture. But to stay innovative and thriving, one must allow opportunities for creativity and growth that can only come by exploring and venturing outside of what is comfortable.

The zone of DM mindset is a mindset in which an individual becomes free in the process of challenging, asking, and questioning the status quo. For the leader, I believe that when you are operating in the zone of DM, you are operating within your talents, executing your genius, and demonstrating the full range of the Success Zone. The Success Zone is where your dreams come alive; this is your sphere of giftedness in which you bring value to others and your organization.

An example of Living and Leading from

Your Success Zone can be taken from Mark Zuckerberg, CEO of Facebook. In June of 2017, he reported a new mission statement for the company, its first major overhaul since creation. He said; "we used to have a sense that if we could just do those things, then it would make a lot of the things in the world better by themselves...But now we realize that we need to do more too. It's important to give people a voice, to get a diversity of opinions out there, but on top of that, you also need to do the work of building common ground, that way; we can all move forward together...The new mission statement is, to give people the power to build community and bring the world closer together." Had the company decided to remain in their initial state; and not challenged their previous model of success; they maybe would have continued to thrive, but would they be winning? The value in winning comes from more than just meeting financial projections, but in expanding to become a meaningful and winning enterprise that is able to incorporate and integrate the desires of its customers. From a top down perspective, transformational leaders set the culture, from the CEO to the management; to those whom they influence; finding value in the message and mission of organization translates volumes. Transformational leaders have also been shown to be critical to influencing: (1) greater alliance around strategic visions and missions; (2) organizational sales increases, market share, earnings and ROI based upon their own behavioral factors; (3) between 45% and 60% of organizational performance; and, (4) greater team cohesion, commitment, and lower turnover (John Antonakis, Bruce J. Avolio and Nagaraj Sivasubramaniam, 2003).

Previously, we discussed that winning enterprises must seek to continually live in their zone of DM in order to remain thriving, and that they must become comfortable with questioning conventional wisdom. This even includes being able to make decisions faster, and being able to be expedient in thinking forward to future opportunities. In authors Brian P. Moran and Michael Lennington's book, The 12 Week Year: Get More Done in 12 Weeks than Others Do in 12 Months. The authors address this very issue and emphasize the importance of accelerating organizational process and creativity for thriving and innovative businesses. They redefine a "year" to be 12 weeks in length and propose that within those 12 weeks, it is possible to disrupt the status quo by avoiding the snags and low productivity tied into annualized thinking. They go on to talk about how great businesses now have 90-day plans, and have abandoned the one-year, two-year, and five-year plans of the past. Although some who are more conservative in their mindset might see this as a slam in the face of stability regarding business growth, it begs obvious questions about the limitless boundaries for creativity, market share, and industry relevance. Being able to remain agile in your thinking, making decisions faster, and bearing in mind the future of decision making allows great opportunities for accelerating growth. Additionally, remaining laser focused on what makes a difference the most also increases the urgency as it entails both innovation and completion of critical tasks.

Much like the agile Cheetah, the leader operating in the zone of DM must consider how maintaining a flexible mindset best complements their individual leadership style. To be a transformational leader, one that is operating in the zone of DM must continually nurture, pursue and cultivate a discipline of maneuverability. In the May 2017 issue of fortune.com magazine, author Cheryl Strauss Einhorn likens certain character qualities of top leaders to Cheetahs, stating; "what makes Cheetahs such remarkable hunters is not their speed, but their ability to slow down quickly. They not only reach 60 miles per hour chasing down their prey, but they can cut their speed by nine miles per hour in a single stride. This gives them an incredible advantage, enabling them to turn sharply, jump sideways, and change directions in an instant. As researcher Alan Wilson explained in a New York Times article, "the hunt is much more about maneuvering, about acceleration, about ducking and diving to capture the prey." Just like cheetahs, we can develop that kind of maneuverability—and better capture each day. By taking calculated pauses, slowing down, and consolidating knowledge; we're more effective when we're back up to speed. We benefit more from being flexible and creative than just rushing non-stop.

When I think about top business leaders that have fostered the zone of DM mindset I think of pioneers like Steve

Jobs, who was quoted as saying; "we're gambling on our vision, and we would rather do that than make "me too" products. Let some other companies do that. For us, it's always the next dream."

When he died on October 5, 2011 at the age of 56, Steve Jobs, the co- founder and Chief Executive Officer of Apple had 241 licenses enlisted in his name or as co-creator. The best and most progressive of these developments have turned out to be irreplaceable to a large number of individuals around the world, devices such as the IPod, IPhone, IPad, and the Macbook.

And other top leaders who have fostered the zone of DM mindset include:

Mark Zuckerberg, founder and CEO Facebook, "...the biggest risk is not taking any risk ... In a world that's changing really quickly; the only strategy that is guaranteed to fail is not taking risks."

Jeff Bezos founder and Chief Executive Officer of Amazon.com and owner of The Washington Post is successful business ventures have made him one of the richest people in the world. He says; "I believe you have to be willing to be misunderstood if you're going to innovate."

Similarly, Sara Blakely, American billionaire businesswoman, and founder of Spanx says; "it's important to be willing to make mistakes. The worst thing that can happen is you becoming memorable."

Cheetahs teach us that success is more about flexibility, maneuverability, and speed. And, just like the great innovators Steve Jobs, Mark Zuckerberg, Jeff Bezos, and Sara Blakely, that we must continually evaluate how to improve and shift the status quo. Great teams, great individuals, you and me; if we're going to be effective at creating zones of disruptive momentum in our spheres of influence; we must remain flexible and swift in our thinking and decision making, and be willing to maintain both a creative and teachable spirit.

So, you might be asking, "how do I achieve a zone of DM mindset and consistently

Live and Lead from Your Success Zone?"

The answer is simple.

Making the commitment and decision to Live and Lead from Your Success Zone means that yes you maintain a zone of DM mindset. But, more importantly, as a leader, it means that you make a decision to be a transformational leader. As a transformational leader your commerce becomes your own credibility and testimony of success to those whom you influence. But, first, you must realize that before you are able to be effective in transforming others, you must first be transformed.

"There comes a special moment in everyone's life, a moment for which that person was born. That special opportunity, when he seizes it, will fulfill his mission – a mission for which he is uniquely qualified. In that moment, he finds greatness. It is his finest hour."

- WINSTON CHURCHILL

So, the answer to the question of how do you consistently Live and Lead from Your Success Zone?

You must be first true to yourself, your values, your mission and your life purpose. You do no one any good living out someone else's mission on your time. You only have one life, and it is well worth living to the fullest!

So to start, success is a journey not a destination. However, to begin the journey to success you must believe that the journey is worth it, and that you are worth the investment. First, to get started you have to identity the importance of your beliefs about who you are, where your value comes from, and how that impacts how you show up in the world.

The foundation of success lies in your belief in yourself. The journey towards success will bring many wavering events and circumstances and *a lot of change* throughout the process, but the one thing that must remain stable is your self-concept. Your belief in yourself will be your source of support in your path towards success.

A critical part of achieving success is working on your self-esteem and self-efficacy, which is your belief in yourself and your understanding of your positive attributes, skills, and abilities. It is important to develop this positive belief system about who you are and what you are capable of because the journey towards success has moments of achievement as well as periods of roadblocks, setbacks, and failures. When your opinion of yourself and your abilities is stable and positive, you will be able to overcome any potential barriers and challenges.

Cultivating a positive belief about yourself and your abilities is a sort of training for future success. *Are you ready for success?* Being able to handle the road to success (and maintain your place as a successful individual) takes strength of character, courage, good values, leadership, confidence, and self-awareness, but first and foremost you must believe that success is possible for you and that you deserve to reach greater levels of achievement, joy, and satisfaction. The *belief* is the precursor - the catalyst to reaching the success that is waiting for you.

Principles of Success: Be, Do, & Have

The principles of *be, do, and have* can serve as your guide to developing and strengthening your belief in yourself. Many of us must teach ourselves these principles during adulthood, as our environments (or societies and others around us) do not promote the cultivation of these principles. Oftentimes, we are conditioned to behave like the proverbial '*flock of sheep*', we are led to believe that we must all strive for the same things, go down the same path in life, and refrain from taking risks and dreaming too much. In order to reach personal success, we must see this pattern and decide that we want something different, *something more for ourselves.*

The principle of *be* relates to your confidence in your ability to achieve your goals, reach success, be who you want to be, and develop into whoever you envision yourself to become. If you think far back to your early childhood, you likely put *be* into practice. Young children tend to believe that they can be what they want in life whether it is a superhero, a dolphin trainer, a pop singer, or an astronaut. We are born with this *belief in ourselves*; however, we unfortunately become conditioned to limit ourselves and doubt our capabilities and the source of this conditioning is oftentimes the *adults* in our lives. As we grow older and begin to find our own answers, we can reignite the *be* principle in our lives by questioning the limitations and messages that society and others have given us, telling us that we can't dream and that we can't be who we want to be.

The principle of *do* means that you can achieve whatever you want in life as long as you believe that you can. *Do* not only consists of the belief that you can put your dreams and goals into action, it also includes the actual execution of your goals. When you establish the *do* principle in your life, you resolve to take action in pursuit of your goals without fear. We all have fears that have limited us in our lives (e.g. *"I'm not good enough/ smart enough/capable enough," "What will other people think of me?"*). These fears usually develop as a result of various life experiences, such as rejection, criticism from others, bad advice, and failure. The *do* principle means that you will create objectives that correspond to your ultimate goal and you will take steps every day to get closer to the attainment of that goal, despite fear or any other limitations. When you apply the principle of *do*, you work at your own pace; and you don't allow any negative outside factors take away your focus and drive.

The *have* principal involves your belief that you can obtain anything you want in life, so long as you put in the work and effort. This principle encourages you to dream and imagine, just as you did when you were a child, the difference is that now; as an adult, you can execute your goals and dreams because you now know that the limitations that you've always known are actually not *real*; limitations are man-made concepts fueled by human insecurity, fear, self-doubt, and a myriad of other sources. Limitations are, in essence, a figment of our own minds and the collective mind of society. They are imaginary concepts that are created to stop us from achieving. But just as limitations are created by the mind, so are your *actions* that will bring down the walls of limitation.

Overcoming Beliefs that Limit You

Surmounting limitations involves breaking down walls that have been built throughout much of your life. This process starts with altering the belief system that fuels these limitations. When you get rid of the baggage of limitations, you achieve ultimate freedom. This freedom will allow you to take risks, increase your creativity, and confront challenges. By developing your self-esteem and self-efficacy, which will allow you to strengthen your belief in yourself and your abilities, you will be able to confront any barriers and limitations that interfere with your success.

The process of overcoming limiting beliefs starts with: (1) questioning what you know; and, (2) questioning why you've always believed (or have been told) that you *can't* do something, or, that something is *impossible;* or, that something is *too hard* to achieve. Those are oftentimes the limitations that govern our lives. When you venture onto the path of overcoming these limitations, you start to ask, "*Why not?*" because if others can do it, *so can you.* This is how you not only cross these limits and barriers, but also erase them from your life. Permanently! No longer are there the days when you first "consulted" your old, *limiting* belief system prior to making a decision or embarking on a goal or task. On your barrier- free path to success, you will only ask yourself *how* you will go about achieving your goals, not *whether* you will pursue them.

How do we get from here to there?

The next step in the process is to look closer at addressing how limiting beliefs impact your pathway to success, the importance of identified goals, and the benefits of accountability on your journey.

"I've missed more than 9000 shots in my career. I've lost almost 300 games. Twenty-six times I've been trusted to take the game winning shot and missed. I've failed over and over and over again in my life. And that is why I succeed."

- MICHAEL JORDAN

Even the best athletes or champions know that wins and losses go together sometimes hand and hand. If you let losses stop you, you will never get to the win.

Take ownership for your part in the process and consider that each day is a new beginning.

Perhaps today you are one step closer to

that win; but you will never know if you don't move forward.

Why You Should Stop Playing The Blame Game

The Blame Game is a game that we ALL play really well, and sadly enough; often. In fact, we have become such masters at it because we have played the game most of our lives. We tend to blame our families, friends, spouses, neighbors, pets, co-workers, our bosses, our kids and so on and so forth. We blame just about everybody for why our lives aren't working the way they are supposed to. And if blaming people isn't enough, we also tend to blame non-living entities such as the government, media, nature, money, etc. for the same reasons. Often times, the very same reasons we feel entitled to an amazing life lead to us not having one at all.

Entitlement is a conditioned feeling that we have in which everyone and everything is responsible for our success. And if we are not attaining any success, it is because someone or something is responsible for our lack of happiness, whether it may be in the home, work, relationships, or play. We feel that our loss of a job, a spouse, health, happiness, income, respect or control is due to something that we don't control. We fail to see that; maybe, the real reason why our lives aren't working is the person who stares directly back at us in the bathroom mirror. Only one person is responsible for the quality of the life you live... YOU. The concept of being responsible is not an easy one to accept. If you want to be successful, you need to be wholly responsible for everything that goes on in your life. You, and you alone are responsible for whether or not you succeed or fail. No one or anything else is responsible. It's not your spouse, or your boyfriend or girlfriend, it's not the weather, your boss, the kids, the traffic, the dog, the economy, the fats in the food you eat etc. It is you!

Being able to take full responsibility for your life gives you power! Because if you believe that you are responsible for the results than you can see, then you can be responsible for the change. What you've created in your circumstance you can un-create. What you've done, you can undo at will. Without seeing yourself as a source of power, you will forever be subjected to the winds of fate. You'll remain a leaf in the wind, a rudderless boat. Unable to control your life, you become a victim of it. So being responsible requires that you quit playing the blame game, stop all your victim stories and your complaints. You need to stop with all the excuses that explain why your life isn't going the way it is supposed to. You have to give up your need to be right, you feelings of entitlement, the fears and the ignorance. You also have to get rid of the emotions and the feelings of being a victim of a past circumstances, of what someone said or did to you that has caused you grief.

You need to assume control of your life and believe that only you have the power to dictate the direction where you life will go from now onwards. What is important is that you believe that what you will have from this point forward in your life is what you get to create for yourself. You are ultimately the creator of your life.

"Twenty years from now you will be more disappointed by the things that you didn't do than by the ones you did do, so throw off the bowlines, sail away from safe harbor, catch the trade winds in your sails. Explore. Dream. Discover."

- MARK TWAIN

We only have one life to live and every day is an opportunity for an extraordinary outcome.

If we stay incapacitated by our fears we are destined to live an unfulfilled life.

Life should not be about regrets.

We as leaders have to be willing to show up in our own lives and in the world living a life of intention and purpose.

Our call to leadership is not only for us

but, is a gift to the world.. Are you walking in your purpose?

By answering yes to that question we as leaders inspire others to believe in their own abilities to do more and dream big.

3 Steps To Get You Moving Towards Your Purpose

Excuses & Procrastination Stunt Your Professional Growth

Although the blame game typically involves finger pointing at other people, situations, or events in your life, ultimately, playing the blame game will only affect *you* and your professional achievements. Blaming is a form of making excuses or procrastinating about what you need to do in order to move forward towards your goals. In addition, if you're too busy projecting blame, then you are likely not focusing on taking personal responsibility for your actions in order to problem-solve and find solutions. The only way to progress is to identify the problem and figure out how your own actions and decisions can solve it.

Don't Be Afraid to Identify What You Want...No Matter How Great It Is

Many people are afraid or hesitant to set goals and objectives due to the fear of failing or fear of being disappointed if they don't reach their dreams and goals. But remember that you can't start on your journey towards achievement if you don't identify where you want to go. Don't be afraid to set the highest possible goals that you can imagine. High performing professionals don't set mediocre goals because they want the best for themselves and they *know* that they can achieve whatever they set their minds to accomplish. These are the ingredients that *make* high achievers and those who break records: *they don't settle for less and they aren't afraid to imagine what others believe is impossible.* If you can *imagine* something then you just took the first step towards making it a reality and a possibility for yourself.

Motivation & Inspiration

An effective strategy for moving out of the *blame-game-excuse- making-rut* is to find what motivates and inspires you. Motivation and inspiration can come from a variety of sources, looking to people you admire or aspire to be like, a negative life experience that you want to make positive, or tracking your own progress towards a goal and striving towards bettering your performance every day. Find sources of motivation and inspiration and look to those sources *every day* to fuel you in your drive towards achieving your professional goals.

"Of all the responsibilities you face in life, this is one of the most important: to identify that area of excellence that can have the greatest positive impact on your career and your income. Once you know what that is, pour all your energies into becoming the best you can possibly be in that key area" -

TurboCoach by Brian Tracy and Campbell Fraser.

If you do not fully understand your strengths, you are not being fully effective – you are selling yourself short. You are essentially living small. As a result, you are not living up to your maximum potential in areas of your personal and professional life with your spouse, kids, co-workers, boss, or business partners. Imagine being twice as effective as you are now. What about five or ten times more effective? It is absolutely possible!

What's holding you back?

"Only those who dare to fail greatly can ever achieve greatly."

- ROBERT F. KENNEDY

I never understood how tied our inner dialogue is to behavior until I had to motivate myself to overcome an obstacle that seemed insurmountable. I remember I was 21 years-old in the last semester of my Masters program at the University of Alaska Anchorage, and was looking forward to transitioning into a doctorate program in California. I knew that this opportunity would change me and my family's life forever. I would be the first in my family to graduate college and earn a doctorate degree. Also, I was committed to serving others and helping individuals as a Psychologist.

However, five months before I had slipped on some ice and fell and broke my leg and tibia. I was out of commission for two months and thought that my academic goals were in jeopardy. It became a battle of will and mental toughness that inspired me. Additionally, I had to ask for help and support which seemed foreign to me in order to accomplish this goal of graduating on time. Believe it or not, I was able to achieve the goal with the support of my family and friends. My brother and mother would wheel me to class in my wheelchair, sit with me and take notes. My professors allowed me to work on some group projects to make up for the lessons that I missed. I was able to get an extension on my Master's thesis from my committee chair. I called the school that I was transferring to and they allowed me an additional month to meet degree requirements. It all came together, but it wouldn't have happened if I hadn't been motivated to achieve the goal. For me, I had to envision myself completing the goal, I had to see myself walking across the stage, getting my degree, and moving on to the next step, graduate school in

California. Also, I had to take the initiative to ask for help, and then identify people that could be of support to me to accomplish the mission.

Sometimes, we as leaders feel as though we have to do everything, which can become overwhelming very quickly. The first step is to consider that your chances of accomplishing a great goal only increases when you expand your reach. Collaborate, ask for help, assemble a team, delegate to others, this allows you to concentrate on what is necessary to remain on mission.

Are you on mission? If not, what do you need to do to get on track and increase your focus?

Stay action oriented, and you will see results!

Mindset Reset

3 Essential Tools to Get You Unstuck

Strategy Change

Getting yourself unstuck and out of your rut may require you to change your strategy and the objectives that you set to reach your professional goals. *Don't get discouraged*. A strategy change is a *positive* thing. Think of it as a necessary *cleansing* of your routine as you strive towards your goals. Oftentimes, after periods of "ruts" comes renewed creativity and opportunity.

Beating Boredom

Getting stuck during the process of goal attainment and achievement can sometimes occur as a result of boredom. When there is much hard work, long hours, and dedication involved in professional achievement, and if there is *repetition* of the process, or *results not being seen right away* can lead to saturation and boredom. You can overcome getting stuck due to boredom by reminding yourself about *why* you are reaching towards your goal. *Find ways to renew your motivation and inspiration.* This can be achieved by talking to others who inspire you, taking a break from your routine, or reassessing your goals and objectives. Boredom can be a signal that you need to reanalyze your trajectory towards your goal and therefore turn boredom into something positive, and make changes that will lead to progress and improvement.

Asking for Help

High achieving professionals do not reach great accomplishments alone. Whether they had partners, advisors, or other associates along the way, one way or another; they reached success because they knew how to find the right people to surround themselves with and unite with others to reach success. Utilizing a network of other professionals can be a great help in getting unstuck because it will allow you to present ideas to others, obtain helpful advice, and look at issues from differing perspectives. In addition, in the process of obtaining help and support from others, you will realize that most (or likely all) high achieving professionals experience periods of confusion or feeling stuck and it is through the process of overcoming this challenge that real professional growth occurs.

My point is that for YOU to be the best YOU can be, as a person or as a leader, you must first understand yourself. You MUST know what beliefs are limiting you and how you characteristically hold yourself back. Then you MUST aggressively endeavor to define and redefine your roles in life to consistently to Live and Lead from Your Success Zone. Take advantage of knowing your strengths. You MUST strive to remove yourself from the pitfalls of mastering the Drift and the Comfort Zone and commit to residing in the Success Zone.

It's Time to Get Down to Business: Goal Setting

"You should set goals beyond your reach so you always have something to live for."

- TED TURNER

I love this part of my job because it really is where the rubber meets the road. Here I'm able to help individuals and organizations to meet and set their own priorities for achievement.

The meaningful part for me is that the goal setting is a marker by which others including the individual leader will measure success. Meeting your goals increases confidence. In some cases it may even provide more opportunities for advancement, inspire team members to set and achieve their own goals, or, it may reinforce commitment in the company brand.

We as leaders demonstrate our

willingness and commitment when we prioritize the things that are important. When we set and meet goals we reinforce for those whom we influence the importance of priorities, achievement, and motivate others to reach their own goals.

As a leader you build trust and credibility when others see you are willing to put forth the effort to achieve success.

Goal Setting

Setting professional goals and specific objectives to reach goals is critical to reaching and maintaining high performance and maximizing results in your career. Goals should be realistic and achievable; but challenging and ambitious at the same time. Goals are the root of a person's personal and professional identity and without them we wouldn't know where we are going or how we will get there.

Keep your goals on track with your true purpose. A lot of people talk about the power of setting goals, but not many about how to achieve them. Yet, it is a fundamental key to a lifelong success plan.

The challenge of course; is that we hear about setting goals so often that we tend to take it just a little bit for granted. When you get to a point where you have heard it so many times; you act like you know all about it. But you need to be careful not to get caught in that trap called the law of familiarity, which is the place where you get so used to setting goals that the process has no meaning.

Setting Goals is Powerful

Why do we need to set goals and focus on them? Are goals important? The answer is that when you set goals for yourself; you create your future in advance. You also form your destiny and shape your life. Whether we know it or not, we all have goals. Therefore, realize that your goals are affecting you. The problem is that some people have lousy goals. Those get you through the day, the week, the month, or help you pay the bills but are not the kind of objectives that inspire you or make you jump out of bed in the morning. Those goals do not create the drive you need to achieve something greater.

You must realize that very few people have particular plans or even written goals. So, when you set goals, I mean real goals; you create the power to grow, develop and expand your success. You must have something out there that is compelling enough to draw you towards taking a step to transform your life.

The first step to goal-setting is to decide exactly what you want. Ask yourself:

What do you want to achieve?

What do you want to learn or what knowledge do you want to gain about yourself?

What do you want to attain at the end of the process?

Who do you want to become?

One of the main reasons most people get discouraged about goal setting, and don't follow through with goal setting, or don't get what they want, is that they aren't clear about what they want to achieve. Others will know what they'd like to achieve, but think the possibility of achieving it is not within their reach so they dismiss the desire as silly.

Remember the zone of DM, don't be a victim to limited thinking! Don't fall into this mindset trap and sabotage yourself!

Set Goals in Every Area of Life

You have to set goals for yourself in every area of your life. Set them personally, emotionally, socially, physically and financially. Create an ultimate aim and decide what you want right now. You need goals regarding who you want to be, how much happiness or passion you desire, and how you want to live every single day.

Start out by asking yourself... What do you want? Is it to create a balanced and successful life? Set 2-3 main goals in important areas of your life as mentioned before, include goals in areas of your life that are meaningful like financial, relationship, career, recreational, professional, and/or educational.

If you have more goals than 2-3, don't put limits on yourself – write all of them down! On the other hand, if writing down 10 or more goals seems like a lot, remember that you can have a mix of long-term and short- term goals. You can also continue to add goals as you achieve others. The process can be tailored to how quickly you want to progress through your success plan. A massive change will occur as you follow through. Your level of confidence will be boosted, and your faith as well as your abilities will be transformed radically.

No matter the number of pages it could take, you should describe everything in detail, even envision what it will look like, when you achieve your goals. And yes, you might instill a lot of limitations or what might seem to you like absurd goals, but if after reviewing those; your goals still make sense to you and they are in line with your life's purpose, you should believe in their realization. You have to design your own road map necessary for success.

Breakthrough Goals

Jack Canfield, New York Times bestselling author of Success Principles, and #1 Success Coach in America talks about the importance of setting breakthrough goals. Break through goals are designed to make you stretch and grow to achieve them. These can be maybe 1 or 2 goals that may take longer to achieve. These goals might be acquiring knowledge, learning a new skill or trying out something that pushes you out of your comfort zone. It might be a goal that is a little frightening to you, such as public speaking. It also helps to set a breakthrough goal that would represent a "quantum leap", meaning that the accomplishment of this goal would change your life and/or your reality. Some examples might be writing a book, winning an Olympic medal, earning a million dollars, speaking before a room of 1000 people.

Once you are clear about what you want, write your goals down and turn each item into a measurable objective.

How to Set and Achieve Any Goal

Perhaps our very human essence is oriented towards the achievement of goals. Even human endeavour is measured by some of its greatest achievements. So, what do you want to achieve? Without a set of key goals, life can become a case of living randomly from day to day. Any goal, whether a small one en-route to achieving a key goal, or indeed a key goal should be S.M.A.RT.

SMART GOALS are:

➢ Specific: state each goal as a positive unambiguous statement.

➢ Measurable: break the key goal down to measurable small steps.

➢ Attainable: make sure it is something that you can accomplish. You have to decide if it is worth the sacrifice to your current work, family and financial commitments.

➢ Relevant and Realistic: make sure it is

physically and mentally possible.

➢   Time bound: aim to achieve the various stages of your goal

according to a preconceived timescale.

Specific - Setting Detailed and Precise Objectives

State each goal as an unambiguous, positive statement. The process of reaching goals includes an initial evaluation, frequent reviews, and progress checks. Goals should be set in specific terms so they appear as crystallized pictures in the mind rather than fuzzy apparitions on the horizon. "I have to lose weight" sounds like a project of enormous proportions with nowhere to start. Setting a more concrete, short-term goal is more effective. For example, decide that at the end of two weeks you will have lost 2 kg. This is a more specific, practical and therefore attainable goal. What precisely do you want to achieve? "I want to be an Olympic competitor" is not a performance goal, it is actually the outcome of a goal. Check that your objectives are specific and not just outcomes.

Measurable - Structuring Goals That Can Be Measured

So you want to walk as a form of exercise... good! What does measured success look like? How far and how often do you want to walk? How would you ascertain that you remain en-route to success and how would you prove this to yourself? You will need to break the key goal down to measurable small steps, like deciding that you will walk 5 km 5 days out of 7. Then find a way to measure progress, for example keep an exercise diary.

Achievable - Is this objective practically possible?

By ensuring that your goals are achievable I am not suggesting that you seek to downgrade them so that they become too easy to achieve. Instead you should check what you are aiming to achieve against the other demands on your time, finances and talent. Keep the low-level goals you are working towards small and achievable. If a goal is too large, then it can seem that you are not making progress towards it.

Keeping goals small and incremental gives more opportunities for reward. Derive today's goals from larger goals.

Set priorities: when you have several goals, give each a priority. This helps you to avoid feeling overwhelmed by too many goals, and helps to direct your attention to the most important ones. Organization and prioritizing are imperative to the success of the true achiever. Attending to the most important items on your "TO DO" list will result in maximum productivity. Less essential items can be ticked off as time permits. Plan the work and then work the plan.

Relevant and Realistic - Are you being honest with yourself?

Is it realistic to learn the piano to concert pianist level? Is it a realistic target for yourself to run a mufti-million pound corporation? Do you have the right personality, can you manage the pressure and worry when things are not quite going to plan? This is the essence of being realistic. Set performance goals, not outcome goals: you should take care to set goals over which you have as much control as possible. There is nothing more dispiriting than failing to achieve a personal goal for reasons beyond your control. If you base your goals on personal performance then you can keep control over the achievement of your goals and draw satisfaction from them. It is important to set goals that you can achieve. Don't waste your time with unrealistic goals, and choose goals that are in line with your life's purpose.

Time bound - has a starting date and an ETA

You should aim to achieve the various stages of your goal according to a preconceived timescale. Unless you build these parameters into your goals you could be paralysed by procrastination and end up more frustrated and un-focused than before you started. Set a precise goal, choose dates, times and amounts so that you can measure your achievement. If you do this, you will know exactly when you have achieved the goal, celebrate your accomplishment, and can take complete satisfaction from having achieved it. Formulate short, medium and long-term goals.

Plotting out your goals in this manner will make you aware of the skills, financial aid, and time you will need along the way. Develop short and mid-term goals to help you build those skills. You will begin to make decisions based on whether or not those choices will be beneficial to your long-term goals. If you just drift along in a sea of choices, allowing the tide of every day life to chart your course, it would only be by co- incidence that you will reach your destination or even recognize it when you arrive. As you take each step, however small, towards your goal, your confidence will grow and solidify.

A Final Word About Setting Goals

In conclusion, make sure that when you set a goal, you know why you are doing it. Making money motivates only so much, but becoming a person who can manifest abundance financially and physically for ourselves and the people around us is much more fulfilling. Having the freedom that money can give or having the ability to give or help others usually motivates more than just earning money.

Remember, the outward symbols of success can all be easily lost. Houses can be lost, companies go out of business, relationships come to an end, people age, fortune and fame fades, but the person that you are, what you have learned in your life, and the new skills you have acquired never go away. These are the true rewards of Living and Leading from Your Success Zone.

"I believe life is constantly testing   us for our level of commitment, and life's greatest rewards are reserved for those who demonstrate a never-ending commitment to act until they achieve. This level of resolve can move mountains, but it must be constant and consistent."

- TONY ROBBINS

When one considers living and leading from their optimal zone of Success it really must be a balance of your talents, areas of giftedness, values, personality, and strengths. But this balance can only come from realizing what your life purpose is and identifying what makes you feel fulfilled.

As a leader, what makes you feel fulfilled

in your work environment? Where does your passion for leadership lie? How are characteristics of this passion mirrored in your personal life? We act what we believe.

For example, my life purpose is to continue to add value to people by helping them to fully maximize their individual potential. I do this by coaching, speaking, and training individuals and consulting with organizations to help bring transformational change to their unique situation or problem.

I believe the characteristic qualities that show up in my personal life have to do with valuing all individuals, having care and compassion for others, and maintaining a desire to inspire and serve others.

How are your talents, areas of giftedness, values, personality, and strengths manifest in your personal and professional life?

What does success mean to you?

Living and Leading from Your Success Zone

John C. Maxwell is a real-life example of someone who has followed these principles. After starting his career as an ordained minister in a small town in Indiana, within a few years, he grew his small church from an attendance of two (he and his wife) to several hundred. He soon discovered his desire to continue growing in his individual capacities and moved on to larger churches. With his disciplined approach he found his Success Zone to be leading others, and he has described his core strengths or areas of giftedness as communication, networking, leading, and creating. He now has founded at least three companies aimed at leadership development, along with a non-profit organization dedicated to training a million leaders worldwide. He has written over thirty books and sold more than seven million copies, including The 21 Irrefutable Laws of Leadership; a New York Times bestseller with over one million copies sold. He speaks to more than 350,000 people every year, and he is now known as North America's foremost expert on leadership.

In Maxwell's journey of discovery, he chose to focus on Living and Leading from the Success Zone by remaining true to his areas of strength. He has built his life and his business around these beliefs, and his accomplishments have surpassed the wildest dreams of most people. Maxwell is not alone in this accomplishment. Many other people who have attained significant success have also followed this pattern: Bill Gates, Warren Buffett, Oprah Winfrey, Michael Dell, Jack Canfield, Brian Tracy, Bill Hybels, T.D. Jakes, Tony Evans, and Mother Theresa, to name just a few.

However, when it comes to our daily work, not everyone can confidently say that they have achieved clear a vision as it regards their life purpose or are working and walking in their area of brilliance every day.

Where are you in this process?

Remember earlier I asked you some questions to stimulate your thinking?

Well, I'm going to ask them again:

1. How much do you love your job?

2. Do you end each workday feeling fulfilled?

3. Are you confident that you are in the right position with the right company?

4. Are you focused on activities that matter to you?

5. Are you capitalizing on your strengths?

6. Are you effective and realizing your full potential?

7. Are you having any fun?

Now that you've gotten this far in the book: how are you able to manifest a zone of DM mindset in your current position and consistently Live and Lead in Your Success Zone? Part of the answer has to do with being able to be clear on what your life purpose is, and having a clear vision about what makes you happy and provides you fulfillment. If you answered 'No' to a majority of these questions, what would it take to make the answers 'Yes'? How much about what you are doing now needs to change?

Almost everyone wants to become successful in their life pursuits. Yet, success does not come as easily as people in general want it to and many people may become discouraged in the pursuit of success. Additionally, sometimes growth requires sacrifice, and frankly, some may not be willing to make the investment.

Here I will discuss four fundamental success principles that are needed for those who want to Live and Lead consistently from Your Success Zone.

1. Love

Love is the first success principle because almost everything that has ever happened in this world happened because of love. We as human beings were created to love, express that love, and grow from love. "We are God's workmanship" (Eph 2:10).

Without love, there would surely be no

single life on this earth. Love creates human beings, who continue to create many other things because of their love. "A man's highest happiness is found in the bestowal of benefits on those he loves; love finds it's most natural and spontaneous expression in giving"- Wallace D. Wattles.

"Do what you love and love what you do" is what successful people always say.

"Your work is going to fill a large part of your life, and the only way to be truly satisfied is to do what you believe is great work. And the only way to do great work is to love what you do. If you haven't found it yet, keep looking. Don't settle" - Steve Jobs.

Confucius probably owns the best longstanding quote about "do what you love." His words were, "choose a job you love, and you will never have to work a day in your life."

Even though the saying has somehow become a cliché, its implication is great and worth implementing. When you do what you love, you're naturally happy and feel fulfilled, and when you love what you do, there's a likelihood you will find ways to continue to doing it in some form or the other for the rest of your life.

That's why love is the first success principle to which you have to adhere to Live and Lead consistently from Your Success Zone.

2. Persistence

Persistence is another success principle. It teaches us not to quit when things gets tough, it also reminds us of the importance of maintaining a mindset of mental toughness. It is correlated with the first success principle called 'love'. With strong love comes high persistence and commitment.

History tells us that Thomas Edison experienced close to 10,000 failures, yet he never believed himself to be a failure. He savored each attempt as an occasion to learn from his outcomes and apply that new learning going forward. Edison likely was in the zone of DM, and he continually challenged his own perceptions of learning to advance to a greater understanding of his own unique gifts that would eventually change the world.

Among all of the values we can have, it seems that persistence is the consistent and fundamental element in achievement for most who succeed, no matter what the task. Persistence requires commitment and does not see failure as an option. It can be a hard road, even though some people make achieving success look easy. Persistence is about ongoing and repeated trials even when there is good reason to quit. Persistence is about the uncomplicated deliberate optimism of knowing your dream is the right thing to pursue.

As a leader, being persistent in the workplace may manifest in you being clear on your purpose and vision. Also, persistence entails being able to consistently demonstrate the zone of DM in your sphere of influence and

Live and Lead from Your Success Zone by being able to confidently state what your wants and needs are, and being able to identify a plan for reaching measurable goals that are meaningful to you.

Transformational leaders require persistence because the leader sets the culture, which then becomes the standard. Maintaining this quality will improve your credibility with those whom you influence, nobody will follow a quitter. If we lack persistence people know that at the first sign of trouble we will falter, and that at the first defeat there is a high likelihood that we will quit. Leaders need to have persistence, not only to be able to drive ourselves forward, but we need to inspire and motivate others to move forward against our own fears and doubts when obstacles surface.

3. Consistency

The third success principle is consistency, which is pretty much about regularity. Success does not come overnight, except for winning lottery or inheriting money. It requires all-in effort from the individual involved. Success is more about accumulation than achievement, process than product. In order to succeed in your life's pursuits, you have got to work not only on the right thing, but also on a regular basis.

Consistency is actually a natural law. If you want to grow a tree, you need to nurture it well by watering, fertilizing, and putting it in a position to thrive. It is not a one-day activity, but a daily activity.

Transformational leaders demonstrate consistency in their thinking, speaking, and behaviors, as observed by those whom they influence. These values, allow insight into the authenticity and transparency of their leadership. When a transformational leader is Living and

Leading from their Success Zone their values and leadership principles are consistent; they realize that trust is a two-way street, they gain respect via their character, and exhibit trustworthy leadership that motivates their teams to perform better.

Consistency doesn't mean being stagnant. Change may be a continuous process for the organization, but the leader Living and Leading from their Success Zone is able to absorb change with consistency and better balance, which will in turn be a benefit to others.

4. Dream

"When the dream is right for the person and the person is right for the dream, the two cannot be separated from each other." – John Maxwell, Put Your Dream to the Test

A dream is one of the most essential success principles because having a dream is one of the foundations of success. Without a dream, success is almost impossible. In easy-to-understand terms, a dream is something that you see or have in your mind which is different from what you see or have now, or a dream may be a mental picture for which there is no physical evidence at the current time. For example, the Wright Brothers dreamed of building an airplane, which had not existed in their generation.

So, what is your dream? It doesn't have to

be as exceptional as that of The Wright Brothers, yet it should be worthwhile enough for you to consider pursuing it.

The best way to search for your dream is to remember what you wanted to become or have when you were a child. When you were young, your dream was inspirational and big because you did not know or care about reality. However, when you grew older, your dream could have become altered because you started to adopt a fear of impossibility. Therefore, take some quality time to search your soul or review what you had thought about when you were young. Dreams don't die; you will get them back.

If you find your passion, you will be able

to connect easier to your purpose. The two are connected, so when you are struggling to find your purpose, get back to what brings you joy and soon you will be making a difference while living a life that you love.

John Maxwell says; "if you're dreaming big, then the size of your vision will surpass your present abilities. Not only that, but your dream will even dwarf your potential abilities. No matter how much you grow and develop, you won't ever be able to accomplish the dream alone. One is too small a number to achieve greatness."

Keep in mind that pursuing your dream may take longer to than you realized and could be harder than you ever anticipated, but it will be far more rewarding than you could have ever imagined. Perseverance maintains your dream. Don't allow disappointments or setbacks to overwhelm you. Instead, remain focused on achieving your dream, and keep a light shining on your intention to accomplish what it is that you have set out to do. Remember to continue to pursue the dream even when things are not flawlessly in place, and be open to how the dream may manifest itself; because it could be different than you had envisioned. Keep your thoughts positive and moving in the direction of success by remembering to celebrate past victories, accomplishments, and positive results daily. This will keep you inspired, encouraged, and help you maintain a realistic mindset about your strengths and abilities.

"A leader is the one, who knows the way, goes the way and shows the way."

- JOHN C. MAXWELL

Transformational Leaders are charismatic. They inspire creativity. They challenge those whom they influence to think, analyze, and come into alignment with a compelling vision. They inspire innovation. Most importantly, their approach to leadership involves taking others along on the journey. They value the contributions of others and create an organizational culture which allows freedom and creativity.

I have always been a fan of creative work environments the energy even feels different. When the focus is on championing innovation while maintaining high energy, high performance, and high creativity you see a different level of commitment from employees. People find more meaning in their work and they feel as though their contributions are valued.

Are you a visionary? Where do you see areas that need to transform? What is your next step? How will you help others see the vision?

CONCLUSION

"One can choose to go back towards safety or forward towards growth. Growth must be chosen again and again; fear must be overcome again and again" - Abraham Maslow.

"You are not here merely to make a living. You are here in order to enable the world to live more amply, with greater vision, with a finer spirit of hope and achievement. You are here to enrich the world, and you impoverish yourself if you forget the errand" - Woodrow Wilson.

I hope you have readily accepted the challenge to find what you're passionate about and to devote your energies to whatever that is. I believe wholeheartedly that if you can find what you're passionate about, you will maximize your individual creativity and will in turn inspire others. Finding your passion and finding what it is in you that needs to come out into the world will be the key to making you a successful leader.

My challenge to you as we close this book is this: do not live your life frantically trying to escape failure. Do not suffer in tortured mediocrity. My challenge is that you live your life self-assured enough to embrace challenges, struggles and obstacles by using what you learn from each event as a stepping stone to success. Reject the urge to avoid and run from fear. Realize instead that fear is a catalyst for introspection and spurs you to move towards growth. I challenge you to release the chains of mediocrity and enjoy a life flourishing in limitless excellence. Continue to be dissatisfied with the status quo and like the mindset of the zone of DM, Live and Lead from Your Success Zone and be comfortable with being uncomfortable.

The goal of this book is to help you realize your abilities and your areas of brilliance, and to challenge you to Live and Lead from Your Success Zone. Part of the process involves helping you to define what to Live and Lead from Your Success Zone means to you, and to guide you through the process of defining your gifts, values, limiting beliefs, and talents. In my 20 years of working with thousands of patients and hundreds of professionals and leaders, constant themes that have emerged have been the importance of gaining clarity regarding 'who I am and what makes me happy'. Gaining a better understanding of individual answers to these questions have been the most beneficial to clients that I have worked with. It is then up to you to take this knowledge, apply it, and work to find how to consistently Live and Lead from Your True Success Zone.

SUMMARY

1. To be successful in life, career, and business, you must be more impactful, effective and efficient than those around you.

2. To maximize your effectiveness and efficiency, you must identify your Success Zone.

3. An individual's Success Zone is defined as their talents, areas of giftedness, values, personality, and strengths.

4. The overlap between your talents, giftedness, values, personality and strengths is how you continue to consistently Live and Lead from Your Success Zone.

5. Once you define your Success Zone, to continue to Live and Lead in this zone you must reevaluate and if necessary, redefine your approach to each of your roles (i.e. personal and professional) to fully access the power of Living and Leading from Your Success Zone.

6. You must spend time investing and developing skills and knowledge in your Success Zone to become even more effective and efficient as a leader.

REFERENCES

Antonakis, J., Avolio, B. J., & Sivasubramaniam, N. (2003). Context and leadership: An examination of the nine-factor full-range leadership theory using the Multifactor Leadership Questionnaire. The Leadership Quarterly, 14(3), 261-295.

Bakker, A.B., Demerouti, E., & Sanz-Vergel, A.I. (2014). Burnout and work engagement: The JD-R approach. Annual Review of Organizational Psychology – Organizational Behavior, 1, 389-411.

Barret, R. (2010). The importance of building a high performance culture. Barret Values Centre, February 2010.

Canfield, Jack; Switzer, Janet (2005). The Success Principles: How to Get from Where You Are to Where You Want to Be. Harper Element.

Collins, J. C. & Porras, J. I. (1994). Built to last: Successful habits of visionary companies. New York: Harper Collins.

Einhorn, C.S.. How Acting Like a Cheetah Can Make You More Productive. Fortune.com, May 2017.

Gallup State of the American Workplace Report (2013).

Hewitt, L., Canfield, J., Victor Hansen, M. (2000). The Power of Focus. Deerfield Beach: Health Communications.

Hiler, K. Cheetahs' Secret Weapon: A Tight Turning Radius. New York Times. com, June 2013.

Inspiring quotes from digital leaders by Ben Davis. Blog Post (Dec 9, 2015).

Kaiser, R. B., Hogan, R., & Craig, S. B. (2008). Leadership and the fate of organizations. American Psychologist, 63(2) 96-110.

Kotter, J. P. & Heskett, J. L. (1992). Corporate culture and performance. New York: The Free Press.

Kowh, L. (2013). Harvard Medical School study. When the CEO burns out. Wall

Street Journal.

Maxwell, John (2009). Put Your Dream to the Test. Thomas Nelson

Maxwell, John C. (1998). The 21 Irrefutable Laws of Leadership: Follow Them and People Will Follow You. Nashville, TN: T. Nelson.

Robaton, A. (2017). Why so many Americans hate their jobs. Money Watch.

Sisodia, R., Wolfe, D. B., & Sheth, J. (2007). Firms of endearment: The pursuit of purpose and profit. Upper Saddle River, New Jersey: Wharton School of Publishing.

Spira, J. B. (2011). Overwhelmed: Work, love and play when no one has the time. New York: Sarah Crichton Books.

Spira, J. B. (2012). Information, Please?, Overload! How too much information is hazardous to your organization. Hoboken, NJ: John Wiley & Sons, Inc.

Tracy, Brian and Frazer, Campbell. (2005)

TurboCoach. AMACOM Publishers: New York.

Wattles, Wallace, D. (2011). The Science of Getting Rich. Soho Books: New York.

AUTHOR BIO:

Dr. Sanchez is a Psychologist and Certified John Maxwell Team Executive Coach, Speaker and Trainer who has specialized in Neuropsychology and Organizational/Business consulting for over 17 years. The Organizational Consulting & Leadership Development component of her practice is devoted to a holistic transformational approach to Leadership. Through the years of her recognized corporate career, she has served in various capacities, in executive, staff, and support level positions, all of which have enabled her to gain a wide range of leadership experiences including, but not limited to: Strategic Operations, Operational Planning, Leadership Development and Training, Human Resources, Employee Retention, Conflict Management, Recruiting and Applicant Screening, Project and Budget Management, Finance Accountability, Sales, Customer Service, Compliance, and Marketing. Her expertise extends to the use of Neurolinguistic Programming

(NLP), Psychology, and other evidenced based practices to help individuals develop and implement strategies that will enhance their personal and professional effectiveness.

Dr. Sanchez has benefited from being mentored by some of the field's most prominent thought leaders including John Maxwell, and she remains extremely passionate about helping to develop the maximum human potential that all people possess. She specializes in Executive & Success Coaching and Business Transformation, and is also a motivational speaker and author. Despite having much of her career centered on the corporate realm, Dr. Sanchez has shared that her inspiration for working with those in the area of transformational change comes from her innate passion for accelerating the growth of others.

Dr. Sanchez spends a lot of her time pouring into others through coaching, mentoring and training. She utilizes her relevant industry expertise and acumen for helping others become successful. She resides with her husband and two children in California. In her spare time she enjoys traveling, singing, listening to music, and spending time with her family.

If you are interested in taking your application of these Success Principles to the next level; or, would like to contact Dr. Sanchez for speaking, coaching, training, or consultation services please connect with her at: avsanchezphd@gmail.com or at www.dravsanchez.com.

www.ingramcontent.com/pod-product-compliance
Lightning Source LLC
Chambersburg PA
CBHW071851200326
41519CB00016B/4334